CHARLIE SONATA

T0348053

Douglas Maxwell

CHARLIE SONATA

OBERON BOOKS
LONDON

WWW.OBERONBOOKS.COM

First published in 2017 by Oberon Books Ltd
521 Caledonian Road, London N7 9RH
Tel: +44 (0) 20 7607 3637 / Fax: +44 (0) 20 7607 3629
e-mail: info@oberonbooks.com
www.oberonbooks.com

A catalogue record for this book is available from the British
Library.

PB ISBN: 9781786820457
E ISBN: 9781786820464

For Bob.

And for Lucy.

Charlie Sonata was first performed at The Royal Lyceum Theatre Edinburgh on the 29 April 2017 with the following cast in alphabetical order:

MO	Nicola Jo Cully
MEREDITH	Meg Fraser
NARRATOR	Robbie Gordon
AUDREY	Lauren Grace
CHICK	Sandy Grierson
JACKSON	Robbie Jack
GARY	Kevin Lennon
KATE	Kirstin Mclean
MR INGRAM	Barnaby Power

CREATIVE TEAM

Director	Matthew Lenton
Designer	Ana Inés Jabares-Pita
Lighting Designer	Kai Fischer
Composer & Sound Designer	Mark Melville
Assistant Director	Eszter Marsalko

Royal Lyceum Theatre Edinburgh

The Royal Lyceum Theatre Edinburgh is Scotland's leading producing theatre. With a strong reputation for excellence in both classical and contemporary work, The Lyceum is committed to developing Scotland's considerable indigenous talents while presenting the best of international drama. In this 2016/17 Season the company is producing 10 high quality productions making it one of the largest producing companies in the UK.

The Company rehearses in its own rooms opposite the theatre, and costumes and sets are designed and built at The Lyceum's workshops in Roseburn.

For more information; please visit lyceum.org.uk

Artistic Director David Greig

Executive Director Alex McGowan

Chair Shonaig MacPherson CBE, FRSE, Duniv

Supported by

ALBA | CHRUTHACHAIL

Royal Lyceum Theatre Company Ltd is a Registered Company
No. SC062065, Scottish Charity No. SC010509

ONE: SOMETHING MISSING

Can this be right?
Is he really going to do this?
He's not sure. Chick counts to three before he opens the door.

Into a consult room in a new hospital.

There is no personality here. This room belongs to whoever is in it.
Mr Ingram is in it.

His face is stone.
His eyes are dead.
He is an important man in this important building.
Chick is suddenly aware that he is now in the private sphere of Mr Ingram,
And that is some kind of breach.
Like a schoolboy in the Head's office.

He may be in his late thirties, but Chick is not a man as Mr Ingram is a man.

In that respect, he's a disgrace.
His skin is wrecked, his hair is thin, he shuffles, he's shabby.
He finds it impossible to be fully awake.
We can smell it.
See it.
This guy's a boozer.

MR INGRAM: *(On the phone.)* It is not at *all* straightforward…I
don't want to know why, I want to know what
happens next… No, after that… *(He listens for a
while. There's a gear change…)* Have you any idea
what would happen to me if that were true?…I
hope for your…It can't be…Don't come here…I
can't help you…Don't…I can't help you….I
won't help you. Not anymore…No, I don't care.
(He hangs up. Sees CHICK.) You can't be in here.

CHICK: Awright?

MR INGRAM: Out you go.

CHICK: Kinda like sounded hingme. Like you were,
             know what I mean, half way through saying
             something or something?

MR INGRAM: Not at all.

CHICK: No, in their room. Know what I mean? When
             you were talking to Gary and Kate. Sounded
             like, what you were on about was only kinda
             half done. Or something.

MR INGRAM: Not at all.

CHICK: They're so like, totally, watching Audrey. Crying
             and stuff. They're no really listening. I don't
             think. Now they know how bad it is an that, they
             can't listen any more…

There they are.
Gary and Kate, in Audrey's hospital room.
Gary and Kate are the same age as Chick.
In normal circumstances you could tell by looking that they're doing very well.
But these are not normal circumstances.
They were woken in the middle of the night by a phone call
And here they are in fucking pieces.

Audrey, their daughter, is sixteen.
She lies silent, eyes closed, in the hospital bed,
Which looks too big, too raised.
The perspective's wrong or something.

It's making her look…kind of…mythical.

CHICK: …and I don't know where Jackson is…

Here he is….

Jackson is alone in his kingdom in the middle of the night.
He's big.
Used to be all muscle.
He can still pull off the old Alpha Male act
If he wants to.

He's in a soft-play centre.
The primary-colour crash mats, ball pools, plastic chutes and climbing nets
Are all in shadow.
He owns this joint.
It's called Castleland.
The only light is from his ringing phone. Which he ignores.
He's scared.
He's hiding.
He sinks into the ball pool.

CHICK: (…) and…and I'm like, totally thinking… Christ, I should be the one that's listening and everything then, eh? Know what I mean? To the details. But I didn't. Can't. Or something. Know what I mean?

MR INGRAM: There was nothing else. You can't be in here.

CHICK: Aye. Could you, like, just remind me but? What you said. I'm no good at, like, remembering and that.

MR INGRAM: Are you a relation of eh…ah…ah…?

CHICK: Naw.

MR INGRAM: There's nothing else. It's all done. Should I get security?

CHICK: Naw. Just. Just tell me it again then. Quickly. You've done all the tests and that…and that's it. Nobody knows anything. Right?

MR INGRAM: They have the details. There's nothing we can do. We'll make her very comfortable.

CHICK: She's only sixteen but. Doesnae seem…

MR INGRAM: I don't understand your insinuation.

CHICK: Eh?

MR INGRAM: They have the details.

CHICK: Waiting game. Aye, I know. I was there, when you told them, sure I was? Shouldnae've been, but…you just fired right in, talking about results and timeframes, and Kate started screaming and Gary climbed up on wee Audrey's bed, pure crying and holding her face and I was like that, shit… I shouldnae be here, man. But how could I get out of that room? I couldn't. Then you just stood up and walked out the door like it was the easiest thing in the world. Follow him! I says. So I followed you. Not just to get out of there. But also, like, cos, it felt like…kinda…like there was something missing. Or something.

MR INGRAM: I assumed you were family. If you have a complaint about my conduct…

CHICK: Oh no. No, no, no Doctor. I mean, no way. Not at all. You were like a…machine in there man. It was me that shouldnae've…I just thought you might've had more to say on the subject. Do you? I wonder? Is there more to say about all this?

MR INGRAM: No. I'm sure it must be very upsetting, but I have many other patients…

CHICK: Are they all sixteen?

MR INGRAM: Of course not.

CHICK: Younger than sixteen?

MR INGRAM: I've treated much younger patients in similar situations.

CHICK: *(Sincerely.)* Jesus. Jesus Christ Doctor. That must be horrible.

(Pause.)

MR INGRAM: Is there anything else?

CHICK: Who was on the phone?

It was Meredith.
She's wearing a ballet dancer's tutu, costume leotard
And "Bad Fairy" make-up
Smeared now.
She has wings!
She's in the waiting area of the hospital, framed by the flashing lights of
the ambulance bay, swithering over whether or not to call him back.
She may be a little older than Chick, hard to tell.
Too old for a tutu and leotard that's for sure.
She's trying, and failing, to blend in unnoticed…

MR INGRAM: No we're not doing that. I suggest you return to your friends.

CHICK: They hate me though. Well, Kate does. I don't know why. I do though. I'm like someone else's dog that ruins her house. They dread this dog visiting, so they do. Mud and blood and stink all over their nice things. Twice a year. For the reunions. But I'm a guard dog man, sure I am? Or I could be. I could protect the children. Sit by their bed. I could wait and wait and if anyone tried to hurt them I'll…

MR INGRAM: Okay. This is finished now.

CHICK: Did *they* ring *you*? I wonder. I'm no being hingme. I'm just wondering. Did your phone vibrate in your pocket during the screaming and the bed climbing and you thought, "Who's this phoning me now? What has this new caller got to say for themselves?" I wonder.

(Pause.)

MR INGRAM: I came in here to make a private phone call. After I left the room. I came in here after that.

CHICK: You phoned them?

MR INGRAM: Yes.

CHICK: Scrolled through 'contacts'…tappity tap…it's ringing?

MR INGRAM: I made the call, yes.

CHICK: Did you mention us?

MR INGRAM: Of course not.

CHICK: Not even a wee bit?

MR INGRAM: No.

CHICK: Not even to kick it off, "Jesus Christ, guess what I've just had to do?".

MR INGRAM: That would never happen.

CHICK: That's a shame sure it is?

MR INGRAM: Don't you know how this works?

CHICK: Aye. No. I mean I'm in hospitals a lot so I am but I don't know how they work. Who are these people that know how hospitals work?

MR INGRAM: We're professionals. What more can we do? You can't have it both ways you know. Either we are professional people who behave as professionals do, or we are not. And then what?

CHICK: No, I mean ordinary folk. Visitors and patients. Ordinary folk who know how hospitals work. "There's no one at that desk after nine son, ring the bell and Margaret will come down from the Nurses' Station on the third floor," know what I mean? God I'm so scared of them. Those people that *know*. Know what I mean?

MR INGRAM: *(Actually he does.)* Mm. We do what has to be done. That's all. There should be no closeness.

CHICK: Aye. See when we were students, me and Gary, we were close. Jackson too. Pissed half the time man, but that made it better. Goes away but. It's like birds on a beach. Sure it is? Off they all go, all at once, flying. I didnae even know they could do that man! Off to get jobs. Nice flats. Girls. Wives. But I'm still here – same as I always was. I just…kinda…stayed. Thought that was…know what I mean…what to do. But it isnae. What good is someone who doesnae change? Someone that just…waits? No good at all.

MR INGRAM: Right, I'm afraid you've lost me, and I have a great number of…

CHICK: It's just not in their blood Doctor. That's the difference so it is. I've got my Dad's blood. I wish *he'd* been in a coma! You should've heard his last words. He called me over. He whispered them into my ear. Appalling stuff. Black, appalling, horrible words. I've never been the same since. Never will be. You'd've laughed.

MR INGRAM: *(His phone rings. He answers quickly. To the phone…)* I don't believe this…well I'm not at the hospital….you're on your own…No…I'll deny it…Of course they'll believe me. I've covered… *(Quieter)* I've considered every eventuality…Well if that is true then tonight is when you finally face the consequences of what you have become...It's too late. I'm not at the hospital...I'm in a cab... I'm not...well find another hero...or better still do something heroic yourself, but I think we both know that's a bloody impossibility, because you are...let me finish...because you are...if you think I'm going to get you more you're...That doesn't scare me in the slightest. *(He hangs up and grabs his coat.)*

CHICK: See before you go Doctor, can I ask you something?

MR INGRAM: You can't be alone in here.

CHICK: I was wondering though...isn't there a kind of hingme? Like, an operation where they could take stuff from me and put it in Audrey? Not blood, cos my blood's poison. But something? Something that will wake her up? A lifesaver or something?

MR INGRAM: Of course not.

CHICK: I don't mind dying.

MR INGRAM: No.

CHICK: I'd like to though. And I know what my last words are going to be, so that's sorted. I've practised it. Cos you can ruin everything with your very last words. They don't tell you that but it's true. Your whole life ruined by the very last thing you say. But I've practised it. So I don't mind dying at all.

MR INGRAM: Maybe you should just go to the pub. Get yourself another drink. There's one across the road.

CHICK: That terrifying one with the wire on the windows and no name? Can you imagine who goes in there? Have you ever been in there?

MR INGRAM: No.

CHICK: I've been in there. I was in there last night. I was supposed to be with my friends. It was time for one of our reunions. But the plans changed when I was already on the bus. I was just leaving London when Gary texted me. I was to come here instead. Because there'd been an accident. And instead of us getting drunk and telling the same old stories we were to be here. We were to find out if Kate and Gary's daughter was going to live or die. A lorry, with the word "Logistics" on the side, hit a car and she was in it. But last night, when my bus got in, and I did as I was told, headed here, I only got as far as the door. I had a feeling. So I texted them back. Said that my bus was late, even though it wasnae, I was right outside, there, standing by an ambulance. I saw that pub. And that was that. Nothing could be done. The details don't help. The stuff I did last night doesnae really matter. Like…I tried to find Mo even though she lives in London and not here…

There's Mo.
She's hanging out of a red phone box like it's a train pulling away.
Peroxide beehive and warm winter coat.
Tough as fucking nails, but smiling.
She has a kind of early 60's air to her.
Not the cool burlesque retro look…
More like a girl from a Tom Courtenay film, or a Smiths cover.
She's waving…

CHICK: (…) And then a woman took my wallet in a doorway. And then a man punched me in the tummy. And then they just walked off together, didn't even run. And then I'm sleeping in a taxi and the driver pulls me out. He goes through my pockets. He says "This is the closest graveyard".

And kicks me in the face. He's wearing slippers but it hurts, man. I try to climb over the railings but I cannae. I put my face onto the cold concrete pavement instead and sleep there, kind of. I walk across the city, no idea where I'm going, but end up back here. I mean, what are the fucking chances! Time travel is non-negotiable. And when I find the room, and see Audrey in that big bed, her hair spread out over the pillow, like someone's tried to make her look more dramatic...I know man. I know for a *fact*. She is never going to wake up. She will forever sleep. And then you came in. But see standing there, listening to you, in that room, giving them the details...More details than anyone could want...It seemed to me like there was still...something missing. Know what I mean? Something important. Maybe it was there once, but it isn't there now. Or maybe it was never there, but it should be there. Just...something missing. But what? Doctor? I'm asking you to tell me what that thing could be? *(Different,)* What's missing?! What is it?! What is missing?!

TWO: THIS IS NOT THE 1990S

Can this be right?
In a bar. The last time Chick was up.
The table has a bloom of menus in the middle and a number in the corner.

Chick is uneasy here.
Too much daylight.
Gary couldn't think of anywhere else to go.

GARY: Hey. Did I tell you I've decide to move back?

CHICK: To Stirling?

GARY: No. To 1994. *(Laughs.)*

> *Gary has a full pint.*
> *Chick's glass is empty.*
> *Gary's self-conscious.*
> *He's said this stuff before, worked on it even.*
> *He's had better audiences mind you...*

GARY: *(Checks his iPhone then sits it on the table carefully.)* Honestly, mate. When I lived there first time round, I was like, yeah 1994 is cool, okay; but no doubt I'll find somewhere better down the line.

CHICK: Know what I mean.

GARY: And I've been around...shit, once upon a time I moved into a whole new Millennium! I had to. For work. But I've come to a decision. See when it comes to the crunch...1994 is actually where I want to spend the rest of my days.

CHICK: 94, man. Ace. Parklife. His n Hers. Dog Man Star. Caught By The Fuzz. *(Sings in a whisper.)* "You and I are gonna live forever..."

GARY: *(Overlapping a bit.)* Right. So I'm there a lot anyway, when that stuff pops up on the shuffle, boom! I'm back. The bassline of *Girls and Boys*... the melody of *Wonderwall*: time travel, Brother. And yeah, I buy the remastered special edition CDs, read the retro mags, new Fred Perry every summer even though I worry it makes me look like a racist or something. But all that commuting back and forward between the decades was driving Kate nuts. Decide! She said. So I have. Time travel it is.

CHICK: Kate's a lovely one. You did very well.

GARY: Mm. *(Slightly put off. Where was he? Oh aye...)*
          So, fuck it. I'm moving back. I have come to the
          conclusion that 1994 has much more to offer a
          young man like myself. Plus Audrey's a teenager
          now. And no court in the land could deny that
          teenagers were better in 1994 than they are these
          days. No court in the land! *(He waits for a laugh.
          It doesn't come.)*

CHICK: *(Looking at GARY seriously.)* Are you still getting
          bullied at work and that?

GARY: *(Quickly, seriously.)* Never said bullied. Side-
          lined. Maybe. No. But, em. *(Pause.)* Mediation
          is...in a larger law firm, Mediation can be...
          em, you know...Most lawyers just love fighting.
          And winning. If there's not a winner and a loser
          they think something's missing. But nowadays,
          with businesses sinking like armadas, marriages
          collapsing into themselves three times over...
          Mediation is more attractive than ever. People
          don't want to go to court. Do it in a Mediation.
          Cheaper too. It's not...it's not a lesser thing.
          It's not. Doing...very, very well. I never said
          bullied.

CHICK: Time travel is non-negotiable. Sure it is?

GARY: Mm? *(Big silence.)* Where's Jackson?

And back we go again.
This time to the student union of Stirling University, 1994.

Chick's glass refills.

Gary and Chick get young without moving from their seats.

*There's a red phone box next to the bar, out of which pops Jackson
in his prime.*

Fit. Sporty. Pint in hand, phonecard in mouth.

JACKSON: *(Spitting it out.)* Phonecard's juiced. So that's me fucked. I need to get me one of those eternal babies, like Chick. Your mum and dad just keep it topped up, sure they do?

CHICK: Take mine.

JACKSON: Your mum and dad? In a shot.

CHICK: *(Handing over a phonecard.)* Be careful what you wish for, Brother.

GARY: My phonecard can only ring my parents' house. Worse than useless. It's like a little plastic guilt generator. I can feel it in my wallet thrumming: "phone your mum and dad, you ungrateful pie. Speak to them! Speak to them!" I use it as a plectrum just to shut it up.

JACKSON: *(Downing his pint.)* Cheers Chick you beautiful boy. I shall be back directly.

GARY: Wait. Are you honestly phoning him, at home, from the pub, to ask for an extension?

JACKSON: I'm a prince in that department. Theatrical Sandy loves me. He's got class that guy and will cherish a call. He comes to the games you know. Stands behind the nets going mental whenever I get a touch. I had to do a presentation right, to introduce my dissertation subject and he was fucking crying at the end of it! He did one of those gradually speeding up rounds of applause you get in films. *(He illustrates.)*

GARY: Did you get a standing ovation?

JACKSON: If you mean, did I have an erection, then yes.

GARY: *(Disapproving.)* Ach. Come on. I take it the nonsense with the cards worked then?

JACKSON: Oui. And it was sensational. So you were wrong, Gaz The Doubter. Gaz The Literal Thinker. Gaz the...fucking...Straight Man. Again.

CHICK: What nonsense with the cards?

GARY: Oh don't get him...

JACKSON: Chick are you taking the piss?

GARY: Someone's taking the piss, but it's not Chick.

JACKSON: Right. For about the fiftieth time... *(Back at his seat, doing his act.)* Imagine this *(The phonecard.)* is a pack of normal playing cards. Well, as I said to Theatrical Sandy, my old grandad could do a trick, right...

GARY: Not your real grandad of course.

JACKSON: Obviously not my real grandad. No, this is a fairytale grandad that I've invented to help stiffen the corduroys of the Head of English.

GARY: Aye, Theatrical Sandy has class all right.

JACKSON: My "grandad" would flick the pack like this, right in front of your eyes...breep...and get you to pick out one card – any card that you happened to notice. Grandad said that the card you were thinking of must have had some meaning or else you wouldn't've picked it, right? So he'd ask you loads of questions: what do you want to be when you grow up, who's your favourite superhero... or whatever, and then he could tell you...for a fact... that your card was the Queen of Hearts.

CHICK: What, because he...loved you or something?

GARY: It's not his real grandad, Chick! He's picturing the guy from the Werther's Originals advert or something.

JACKSON: *(To CHICK.)* I've said it before, but it bears repeating…you have a really beautiful soul, old boy. That's your gift.

GARY: *(A toast.)* A soul the size of a buffalo's heart! *(To JACKSON.)* Unlike some people. For whom life is an exam to cheated.

JACKSON: He guessed the card, not because he loved me, but because there were ten Queen of Hearts in the pack. Your eye picks up on the repetition. See? It's a purely physical reaction. Way beyond cognition. It's a trick. But, as I said to Theatrical Sandy, there is an important point to made here…

GARY: I doubt it.

JACKSON: …And it forms the central thesis of my dissertation.

GARY: What's it called again? I could do with a laugh.

JACKSON: "Kurt Vonnegut's Theories of Time Travel in Relation to the Fundamental Tenets of Britpop".

GARY: "Fundamental Tenets of Britpop"? See…one of the many problems I have with that is…there are no "Fundamental Tenets of Britpop".

JACKSON: Oh really? "Tenet One: a rejection of America as the prime cultural source; Tenet Two: a playfulness in relation to class definition; Tenet Three: a return to un-deconstructed ideas of masculinity but with a heightened awareness of the joy inherent in women-hood i.e. *Loaded's* New Lad meets the *Girlie Show's* Ladette. Tenet Four…"

GARY: Okay, okay…stop.

JACKSON: Eh, sorry Gary what were you saying there?
            You're a...what was it...soulless son of a...sorry I
            missed it?

GARY: I was saying...see the amount of actual work
            I have to do in my course when you arts guys
            just...Well come the millennium I will be living
            my life on solid ground and laughing my ass off.

CHICK: Jackson...do you mean time travel like...bands
            all sounding like the Beatles and stuff?

            Things are changing...

JACKSON: *(Getting up.)* Yes! That is what I mean, Chick.
            The 60s is exactly what I mean! The 60s were
            so important to the cosmic order of life, here in
            the West of Earth, that the great Croupier In The
            Sky has fixed the deck to make sure we get the
            point. But do we get the point?

GARY: No. Cos it's bollocks.

JACKSON: The point is...This is not the 1990s. This is the
            1960s...*again!* It's the same time...the same
            card...repeated. It's something to do with what
            we want to be when we grow up and who our
            favourite superheroes are. The same things
            will happen, just as they did in the 60s, but to
            us! Time is a deck of cards, stuffed with the
            decades...but there are two 1960s in there...
            at least! Way beyond cognition, man! Vonnegut
            knew it. His stuff is littered with it. Cosmic
            doubles, exchanging destinies, real life time
            travel, time folds, time waves; the most vital
            moments in life, the most absurd moments,
            happen again and again in slightly different
            forms, calling to us until we get it right. And
            we're slap bang in the middle of the big one!
            I can literally feel the electrical charge in the

ether. We're getting a second chance here boys. Only this time everything's better, because we can learn from the mistakes.

GARY: *(A list.)* Don't boo Dylan when he goes electric; don't ask the Hell's Angels to do your security; if you're an American public figure of any note a bullet proof vest is a good idea...

JACKSON: Exactly! It's a gift. Just being alive now is a gift! And because it's bolstered by the past, everything we do is doubly good.

CHICK: "Good, good, double double good".

JACKSON: I mean you only have to look at the shit bands that have suddenly got game since the time travel kicked in...Radiohead, Paul Weller, The Manics, Christ even U2 are good nowadays, and all because the 60s are shooting through their veins like fucking heroine. And that's just the music. Films, TV, the novel, comedy, art, fashion... you can see it there too. Vonnegut got the arrow in the bull's-eye! Just wait until you get a load of the political revolution coming our way. Oooooh man! It's going to be sweet. This is a hell of a time to be young, boys. Plus we've got Euro 96 coming up which is going to be amazing.

GARY: Actually, that *is* going to be amazing.

JACKSON: Except for the fact England are going to win it.

GARY: 1966 and all that.

JACKSON: Yeah, but what can you do. Time travel is non-negotiable.

(Beat.)

CHICK: I'm in love again. And I don't know what's going to happen.

Gary and Jackson share a secret smirk.
Did Chick see that?

THREE: TO SEE HER LIFTED

Can this be right?

Chick is back outside the door of the hospital consult room.
Is he coming out…or going in?

Is he going to do this?
Again?
He has to know.

He goes in.

Empty.

He must have already spoken to the guy.
Yeah, that's right.

Of course it is.

As he closes the door he sees the rest of the waiting room…

It's full of…
Ballet dancers.
They are fully made up
Dressed as…Fairies.

Chick watches them as they stretch and chat.
Some are running through segments of a routine.
Some are on their phones or flicking through magazines.

It's hard to know if something like this is real or not.

He can feel someone staring at him.
Who is it?

Meredith.
She stands apart from the others.
In the corner
Shunned by the ballerinas.

She's waving him over.
Chick follows orders.

MEREDITH: He's gone. He walked right past you, love. Right in front of your very eyes. Out of that door, to the car park. He has a Mercedes car. I can't remember the numbers involved but I do know that it's too young for him – a convertible. And he has children, so there's that. Now, I don't want you thinking that he turned invisible or something along those lines. What actually happened was that he turned *you* invisible. He can do it like... *(snap.)*...that! He did it to me too. Looked right at me but... *(snap!)* He vanished me. He's gone now so we're visible again. Are you one of his patients?

CHICK: No.

MEREDITH: Are you sure, love?

CHICK: No. Aye. I'm not his patient. The doctor, you're talking about? Naw. I'm not his patient.

MEREDITH: Whose patient are you?

CHICK: I'm no one's patient.

MEREDITH: Are you sure, love? I think you probably are somebody's patient are you not? Even just a little bit?

CHICK: No. Kinda. Naw. Well...No here. In London, I am. A little bit. It was a toothache, but it went kinda...know what I mean. Septicaemia. Spread or something. They said there's always a danger but I'm like that...Nah. There's a reunion. Know what I mean? Cannae...cannae be a patient. Not now. Are *you* his patient?

MEREDITH: No. I'm his sister. *And* a visitor. We're all anxiously awaiting the news. *(She gestures at the dancers.)* As you can see.

CHICK: Oh right.

MEREDITH: You will have heard that The Latvian choreographer Sim Bree has been poisoned.

CHICK: Has she?

MEREDITH: He has, yes. And nobody knows who did it. *(Mouthing the words in a dramatic whisper and pointing at herself.)* It was me. *(Pulls an exaggerated "I'm really worried" face.)*

CHICK: Are you a ballet dancer?

MEREDITH: No.

CHICK: I mean...eh...how come you poisoned a guy?

MEREDITH: Sssh! Ballerinas are largely unhinged creatures. They're finger pointers, love. It's in their training. These little bitches would make it sound like what I did was against the law if it meant them climbing the ladder even just a rung.

CHICK: But...

MEREDITH: That's why I made sure they brought him here. What a palaver with the ambulance man...I told some incredible lies, so I did. I made some promises I don't know if I can keep. But here we are now. Safe I thought. My brother is a big wig in this building. He'll cover my ass should the little bitches start with their finger nonsense. But no. Little Bro crapped out in the usual style. I'm on my own tonight. Again. Surprised? No.

CHICK: Right. I better go and...find my pals.

MEREDITH: Look love, it's very straightforward. I'm staying with my brother and his wife, Hannah - who is ten times the human being he is by the way; she is a goddess that woman; the clothes she has! Anyway I'm in their annexe while I prepare the case against my ex-husband for partial custody of my child whose name is Tarra. To that end I have been working part-time in the marketing department of the ballet, which consists largely of booking flights and hotel rooms but I don't mind it, I really don't. I'm costumed in this manner because I was having sex with the Latvian choreographer Sim Bree inside a castle on the set of his latest show. It's part of his ritual, if you will, to do that kind of thing, on set, as the audience file in on the other side of the curtain for press night. We've had hidden sex many times, in many parts of the theatre, but on this occasion it became apparent that the Latvian choreographer Sim Bree was under the impression I was someone else entirely. Her, in fact. Her name's Leanne. *(She points at a dancer who is wearing the same costume.)* So I got quite annoyed and poison got in his lucky wine and here we are. He's not going to die. And if he does I'll get away with it.

CHICK: Right. See you later.

MEREDITH: Wait a minute. I saw the way he looked at you.
            When he turned you invisible. It was the same
            way he looked at me. When he turned me
            invisible. So maybe... we're the same.

CHICK: We're not.

MEREDITH: Maybe deep down we are?

CHICK: I dunno.

MEREDITH: I think we might be.

CHICK: I don't.

MEREDITH: Look, I think I might need some help tonight.
            An ally. A brother. Or...long shot...maybe I
            need to be heroic. In some way. That's a concept
            my mind keeps hooking on. Would that be
            something you could help me with?

                    Chick is struck by that.

CHICK: Yes.

                    And now
                He's struck by a fist.

Chick falls to the floor, stumbles to his feet, scrambles, runs...

                    Into a phone box.
        He jams the door shut with his arms and feet.

            Can this be right? Where is he?

                He's in London.
                He's at his worst.

Panicking, terrified...nightmarish. Fuck.

Mo and a Man race after him.
Clawing, banging, grabbing at the phone box door.
There is something of the dog in both of them.

Mo is hysterical, partially undressed, gnashing at the glass.
The Man is licking his chops.
Calm, but excited. Smug.
Like someone whose plan is coming to fruition exactly as he knew it
would...

CHICK: I'm phoning the police!

MO: Fuck you can phone the police! I'm fucking
            phoning the police! It's me that's phoning the
            fucking police. You fucking...didnhe? Fucking...

CHICK: Help! Help me!

MO: Fucking rapist!

CHICK: I never!

MAN: Right mate. Mate, listen, mate. Listen. You
            hearing me? How can you phone the police
            right, if it's Mo that was the one attacked? Do
            you know what I mean though? It don't make
            no sense mate.

CHICK: It wasn't! Yous attacked me.

MO: He's a fucking...

MAN: *(MO.)* Shut up a minute will ya.

MO: *(CHICK.)* You're fucking dead!

MAN: *(CHICK.)* Do you see what I mean though mate?

31

MO: He fucking…robbed me. Raped me and everything.

CHICK: I didn't! I love you!

MAN: Mate, mate, mate…Calm down. Okay. Think of it from my perspective, okay? I ain't ever seen you before 'cept down at the graveyard, hanging about, watching from a distance, right…

MO: He's the one come down there to us! He's the one doling out booze and gear just to fucking worm his way in. How he say I attacked him?! He follows me down there day after fucking day…like a fucking…

MAN: And next thing I know, I come in, she's screaming, you're running. Something's not… know what I mean.

MO: He's a fucking psycho. Fucking…you're fucking dead for this. Understand. Tonight! Fucking tonight you die!

MAN: Shut the fuck up Mo! Fuck sake.

CHICK: Naw. Naw. You're my girlfriend but.

MO: You're not right in the fucking head.

MAN: Mate listen to me. How can she be your girlfriend if she's my girlfriend? Know what I mean. It don't add up.

CHICK: Naw…we…it's been…we've been…we were going to a wedding.

MO: I'm married anyways you fucking dick.

MAN: Think about it, right…no mate…just think about it. The police, right, who they gonna believe? You're a fucking…no offence and everything… and I'm not being funny…but you're an alcky jock tramp or something. And there's two of us, yeah? So. It's us innit. And she's screaming that she wants you dead for this...

CHICK: I didn't do anything to hurt her...

MAN: ...and, know what I mean, there's people here who will. You've seen them...she knows. Those graveyard goons are so fucking gone they'll do you for a hit, man. They'll do you for a flash of her fucking tits, man.

CHICK: I didn't do it though. We were in love! I have poems to prove it!

MAN: I don't want to see any cunt done in. That shit is messy. Know what I mean...

MO: We'll spike you, fucker and watch you sleep!

MAN: ...I think the way out of this hole you've dug is to use that phone. Now, you says to Mo your parents was rich, right. Loaded you says. Okay? I think, all things considered, if you get them on the blower right now, get some cash sent down here quick as a flash, then I can make this good. No need for the fucking pigs, mate. Ain't the way for us is it? Not natural. And no need for junkie zombies lunging at you, thorns in hand neither. I think I can sort it but I have, what they call, conditions. Now you ain't never to come down that graveyard again. Okay. That's the rule. Know what I mean. It's non-negotiable. And obviously you can not never...*never*...talk to my Mo again. But all things considered, at least you ain't dead, mate. Know what I mean.

CHICK: They won't give me any money.

MAN: You ain't even tried mate. Blood's thicker than water and everything.

CHICK: I can't.

MO: We ain't fucking leaving until you do.

MAN: She's right mate. We ain't. Don't be a hero mate.
           Cos, you know something, and I'm not being
           funny…but you can't be a hero on account of
           what you've done. You're the fucking villain in
           this mate.

CHICK: All my stuff is back there.

MAN & MO: *(Kicking and slamming the phone box, rising in
           volume.)* Speak to them! Speak to them! Speak to
           them!

Can this be right?
Chick is outside the consult room of the hospital.

Again.

No.
Different room.
Meredith's here too.
This is Audrey's room.
Meredith says…go on.
Count to three, knock and go in…

Audrey is exactly as we saw her last.
Same fantastic hair; same broken, porcelain, face.
Kate has fallen asleep holding her daughter's hand.

Chick is looking for something.
His bag.
It's over there behind Kate's chair.
Tiptoe though.

Meredith is hypnotised by Audrey.
Meredith understands.

MEREDITH: *(Whispering.)* I know what we need to do.

CHICK: *(Whispering too.)* Get my bag back. There's a pub I know. Couple of steadiers.

MEREDITH: No. We can't go. I know what the story is. I know how to be heroes in this story. I know who the villain is!

CHICK: Accident innit. Know what I mean. Once we've got a glass in our hand we can get hingmied. Focused an that. Analyse our strategy.

MEREDITH: I've just realised that you haven't asked me the most important question of all.

CHICK: What *is* your name?

MEREDITH: Meredith Ingram. But not that. Something else. The most obvious question. The question which must have been on the tip of your tongue from the very moment you laid eyes upon me.

(A few big beats…)

CHICK: Em…Are you…actually a…?

MEREDITH: "What show is the Latvian choreographer Sim Bree currently producing which requires costumes such as this"?

CHICK: Oh aye.

(Another beat.)

MEREDITH: Ask me then.

Kate's stirring.
Chick dreads waking her.

CHICK: Em…what show is…em…

MEREDITH: Latvian choreographer…

CHICK: Latvian choreographer…em…simple…

MEREDITH: Sim Bree. Never mind. Prepare yourself. Our mystery will open like a rose revealing petals within petals and the answers will be pollen on our wings. Everything. Wow.

CHICK: Know what I mean.

MEREDITH: *(Dramatic build-up.)* Our show…is…Sleeping Beauty! *(Does a "Ta Da!" at Audrey.)* You need to kiss her. If you kiss her she'll wake up and everything will change.

Chick runs that through his head.

CHICK: It won't. Nothing will change if I do that.

MEREDITH: I'm Carabosse, love. I'm the jilted fairy. It was my magic put this poor cow to sleep. I know. Go on! Kiss her.

CHICK: *(Looks at KATE.)* Once, like, a few years ago or something I was staying at Gary's, right, and Audrey had been at a party and she came in and she was drunk. She was like, I dunno, 13 or something. And they went mental. And I was like, but we did that too, know what I mean. And Gary said, "So fucking what?" And I said, "well, if we did it…it must be normal". And Gary said like, it's the normal things you have to worry about. Know what I mean. Then Kate said she didn't want Audrey to be like us. Because we can't stop. She said that's the only reason we're pals. When we drink we can't stop. Gary said it was the other way round. We can't

stop *because* we're pals. But they did stop. They
can stop. It's me that cannae change.

MEREDITH: I'm just wondering why you're telling me this
now, love?

CHICK: Well...hingme. Audrey collapsed on the kitchen
floor and Kate just picked her up. I mean, look
at the size of her. Just picked her up with no...
hingme...no strain. There was no strain. It was
magic...to see her lifted.

MEREDITH: Kiss her.

FOUR: CLOSE

In Gary and Kate's kitchen, not that long ago really.

It's big and cool.
Behind the long wooden kitchen table the entire wall is a blackboard.
There are quotes and scribbles and drawings all over it in different coloured
chalk.
In huge letters, right in the middle, someone has written
"WE NEED..."
And under that,
"COMFORT".

Chick is being sick in the sink.
When he's done he sets to work.
Quickly, efficiently and with little or no panic,
He removes all traces of vomit.
He has been through this manoeuvre on an almost daily basis for years and
years.
This is business.

When he's done – just in time!
Kate comes in with Audrey, both carrying shopping bags.

Kate looks stylish. She has a sparkle in her eye.
She doesn't hate Chick.
She hates the fact that Chick is the only person on earth who makes her feel uptight.
She knows it's all coming from her side, but that just makes it worse.
She hears herself overcompensating.

Audrey is well used to being around adults.
She has the zing and excitement of a clever teenager who has just recently worked out that the world is sitting there waiting on a girl like her to come along
And tear it apart at the seams.

KATE: *(Singing.)* Good morning, good morning…you screamed the whole night through!"

CHICK: Awright.

AUDREY: He screamed once, mum, leave him alone. Good morning Charlie Sonata. *(She kisses CHICK.)*

Audrey just about hides the fact she can smell it…

CHICK: Sorry.

KATE: What time did yous get to bed?

CHICK: Oh. *(Giggles.)* Know what I mean. Two or something.

KATE: *(Does the wrong answer buzzer noise from Family Fortunes.)* It was two when I went up and *Withnail and I* was just getting going. I see my dad's Christmas whiskey has been tanned. Gary will get his cubes booted for that later, let me tell you. I'm joking of course. Tell me something, does the conversation change when I go up, or is it still just Jackson and Gary arguing about bands they both like? What happens when I go?

CHICK: *(Trying to joke. Hits it too hard though.)* Life! We talk about I mean. All the…know what I mean…all the big…hings an that *(He giggles a bit.)*

KATE: I take it my husband is still in his scratcher then?

AUDREY: Oh my god Mum you said "husband" and it wasn't ironic!

KATE: So I did! The times they are a changing right enough. *(To CHICK, as if explaining a joke to a child.)* Audrey's father was a…well…

AUDREY: Arsepiece.

KATE: I was going to say an iconoclast, but yeah, arsepiece is fine. He didn't take any standard definition of the word husband particularly seriously, so consequently, neither did I. But now I have a new husband and hey - let's take off those inverted commas and party!

AUDREY: *(To CHICK as she unpacks the shopping.)* Did Dad tell you about his screenplay?

CHICK: Gary?

AUDREY: Yeah. I'm calling him Dad now just to make him feel weird.

CHICK: Naw. Screenplay. Em…How come? Or…

KATE: Well. It's a hobby really, Audrey. I'm not sure he's telling folk.

AUDREY: Why not? It's going to be awesome. Do you want to hear the pitch?

                          Oh no.
                       Chick freezes.

AUDREY: Are you okay?

He's going to be sick again.
He has a system though.
He can control it with breathing, swallowing and riding the wave.
Moment by moment.
It'll pass.

AUDREY: *(Looking at KATE, who mimes "keep going".)* Right.
               Okay. It's a horror film right, but like, more
               like a thriller? But a psychological-thriller with
               horror undertones?

CHICK: *(Barely.)* The Undertones. *Teenage Kicks.* 78.
               Buzzcocks. *This Year's Model.* Patti Smith. *(Singing*
               in a whisper.) "There's a darkness on the edge of
               town…"

AUDREY: *(Overlapping.)* It's called "*Close*", right? A single
               father and his two year old daughter live in a
               tenement building in Glasgow, right, and one
               day they're at the bottom of the stairs loading in
               the shopping bags from the car, you know, into
               the close…

KATE: *(The shopping.)* Where does he get his ideas from
               I wonder? *(Putting the kettle on and shouting off.)*
               Gary! Do you want a quadruple whiskey and a
               pair of pints, or just a coffee? *(There's an offstage*
               death-rattle from Gary. Kate rolls her eyes.) Ah, the
               mating call!

(KATE exits.)

CHICK: Know what I mean.

AUDREY: *(Continuing to CHICK.)* There's one bag left in
               the car, so the dad goes back to fetch it, shutting
               the front door behind him - leaving his little girl
               with the rest of the shopping at the bottom of the
               close. But when he gets back…the little girl is

gone! The back door is bolted shut and the front door was locked. There was nowhere for her to go! Except…right?

CHICK: *(Becoming horrified.)* What?

AUDREY: She must be in one of the five other flats in the close! Someone in one of the other flats must've taken her! But when the police search the neighbours' homes…nothing. Not a trace. But the dad knows…one of these people – people he's living right alongside - must have his daughter. Is it the single businessman? Is it the student guys? The Muslim family? The friendly old lady with no children of her own? Where is she?

(Beat.)

CHICK: Where is she?

AUDREY: Ah, you'll have to wait till it comes out.

CHICK: When's it coming out?

AUDREY: He's not written it yet!

CHICK: Oh yeah. That's em… *(Giggles. Then a big pause. During which he gets really itchy.)* Ooft. That's pure freaking me out, man. Close. I hope it's the businessman that has the kid though. Do you not? You can do stuff to him. It's allowed.

AUDREY: What happened to your girlfriend? The one you wanted to bring to mum and Gary's wedding?

CHICK: *(Defeated.)* Nothing. *(Another silence. Change of subject.)* What's this? Know what I mean. *(He points to the blackboard.)* "We need comfort." Did you write that?

AUDREY: *(A bit confused.)* Yeah.

CHICK: It's beautiful. Is it a poem or one of they…other kinda hings?

AUDREY: No. It's not a poem. It's a shopping list.

CHICK: Is it?

AUDREY: Comfort is a fabric softener.

CHICK: Is it?

AUDREY: It just means we need to get some more fabric softener.

CHICK: Right. *(He giggles a bit. Then he's quiet for a little while. Then…)* Cos see sometimes I…I…wish that…I think that what's missing is…

KATE: *(Entering. Slightly changed. More serious…)* The thing is, I'm not a harridan. He forces me into it. We used to play badminton and it was just the same. He'd bat me from corner to corner and he'd be standing in the middle looking effortless while I was like that… *(Acts it out a bit.)* I don't care what time you went to bed or what you were doing. Honestly. I don't even know why I asked you that.

AUDREY: I know what they were doing. They were telling the same stories they always tell. It's funny. The exact same anecdotes, in almost the same order. Over and over and over again. Stories you already know. Why do you do that? Can you go back and change them, even though you all know the truth? Is that allowed?

KATE: Audrey's going to try for Stirling, Chick.

CHICK: Are you, Audrey? That's so cool.

AUDREY: Maybe.

KATE: It's all different now though. We were through for a day trip last year. They've bulldozed all the bars. There's no red phone box in The Long Bar. In fact The Long Bar is a coffee shop and computer lab these days. Young folk just don't drink like you guys did.

CHICK: No?

KATE: How can they? They've no cash. They all work. You lot dossed your way through Gary says. And there was me busting a gut on my business, paying my taxes and wasting my youth getting married and having a baby.

AUDREY: Thanks for that Mum.

KATE: Oh sorry darling, did I not mention that you've ruined my life and destroyed my looks?

AUDREY: Daily. Any advice for Uni, Charlie Sonata?

CHICK: *(Giggles. Shrugs.)* Just...I dunno. Spirits?

AUDREY: Spirits?

CHICK: If you get into spirits, it's a stronger hit, so, know what I mean. A bottle's dearer to start with but it lasts longer with a bit of care. Not brandy though. If your boyfriend's on the brandy, walk away. For you, I'd say, vodka. 1-2-3, in your room before you head, straight back, all three, hit the pub a little later maybe, when your buzz is on, surf that, so no need for a biggy from the bar – top it up with two doubles as soon as you hit the club, one to knock back, one to sip... and that's your night really. Hardly spent a hing. Watch the mixers. OJ rots your gut, Coke rots your teeth, Red Bull rots your confidence, know what I mean. Straight up. Ice. Boom. Stay healthy, man.

Audrey laughs.
Kate laughs.

And Chick is devastated.

JACKSON: *(Coming in from the garden. He's been for a run.)*
What's the gag?

KATE: You've just missed Chick giving the worst advice
ever. Have you been running Mr Jackson?
That's very impressive. No hangover then?

JACKSON: My hangovers are largely emotional affairs
these days, Kate. Morning toots. *(Ruffles Audrey's
hair. As a gesture it doesn't quite work. He soldiers
on …)* Sometimes it's the blues, sometimes it's
regret, but mostly it's dread…the dread of what
happened, the dread of what's about to happen.

KATE: Well, I hate to spoil your dread, but what
happened was you stayed up all night wishing it
was the nineties. Business as usual.

JACKSON: Not me.

KATE: Aye, right.

JACKSON: Nah. I quit the booze early doors. I was on
ginger beer. And as for the nineties: blues…
regret…dread. I have an emotional hangover
from that decade.

KATE: *(Teasing.)* Ach, do you just get a pure beamer cos
you had a street party when Tony Blair got in
and a funeral when the Spice Girls split up?

JACKSON: For the record… I am not ashamed of either of
those events. *(He winks or shakes his head, letting
AUDREY know that he's joking. He helps himself
to a glass of water. The following is for AUDREY.)*

See you're lucky, you guys are plugged into the world. We had no computers then.

KATE: We did so.

JACKSON: Word processors. And only the poshos. No internet I mean. We were the last generation of teenagers who wrote letters to each other. But we weren't plugged in. I didn't read any newspaper apart from *Melody Maker* and the *NME*. There was a TV room in the halls of residence...I was in there for *Top of the Pops* and *Match of the Day* and that was it. So do you know what I think of when Gary starts giving it his Britpop pish? The Balkans. The Balkan War. That stuff actually happened...just across the water there... and it passed us by. Or, we passed it by. Have you ever read what went on there? Like, what actually happened? It's...it's a horrorshow. And what were we doing? Sitting of the floor of some kiddy-on squat spliffing up and drinking wine from the bottle arguing about Chris Evans and Guy Ritchie. Nah, I don't buy all this retro stuff. It's cherry picking. Retro is the opposite of history. Write that down.

KATE: So you're not coming with us to see Morrissey then?

JACKSON: Don't be ridiculous woman! Of course I am. Morrissey's different. *(JACKSON takes his sweat shirt off. He has a tight T-shirt on underneath.)* Okay if I grab a shower?

> *Kate and Audrey try not to stare.*
> *Too late.*

KATE: *(To deflect.)* Aw naw, Audrey, look. Uncle Jackson thinks he's the love interest in a chick flick. It's

a pure shame int it? He thinks he's the hunky
singleton here to set us free with our lust.

Jackson can take a joke.
But this level of irony is lost on Chick.
It makes him very unhappy
And a little frightened...

AUDREY: Do you think we should tell him the truth?

KATE: What, about his fatness? No, never. It would
            break him. It's best just to pretend you fancy
            him, it's the only language he understands.
            (Putting on a voice.) Oh my god Jackson did you
            nick that T Shirt from a wee boys' PE kit or is
            it just that your massive pecs are distorting my
            sense of perspective?

AUDREY: Uncle Jackson I'm confused, how can a man of
            67 have a body like that?

KATE: And it's not surgery Audrey. That's one hundred
            per cent natural. This physique was hard
            earned from a simple routine of bodybuilding
            supplements and illegal hormones bought on the
            internet and injected into his groin, just as nature
            intended.

AUDREY: And it's in no way covering up for something,
            that's what I love about it.

KATE: Exactly. If anything it's a sign that he's a
            rounded, emotionally balanced and sensually
            attentive man. That's the attraction actually.

JACKSON: All right shut up. I'm going for a shower.

AUDREY: *(Pawing at JACKSON, laughing.)* Mummy, would it
            be okay if I had shower with Uncle Jackson?

KATE: *(Laughing.)* Get in line missus! Oh God, I can't control myself!

                            For Chick
                      This is all wrong.

CHICK: *(Snapping.)* STOP IT! Stop. See that. That's fucking...know what I mean. Gary's a kind boy. You have to stop all this, man. Stop... all of it!

JACKSON: Woah, Chick. Settle down, Brother. It's a joke.

CHICK: No. No. It's no a joke. It's...STOP IT! STOP IT!

KATE: *(Angry.)* See, this is exactly why...

CHICK: *(A sudden pain in his mouth. He screams, holds his head and drops to his knees.)* AAAAH! *(AUDREY goes to hold him but he's sick. She screams and springs away. CHICK tries to wipe away the mess.)*

                Gary comes through the door...
                    Can this be right?

                Into Audrey's hospital room.

                He's carrying two cups.
      He sees Kate fast asleep holding Audrey's hand.
  He sees a stranger – Meredith - dressed as an evil witch fairy
    And Chick leaning over about to kiss Audrey on the lips.
                   Jackson's gone.

CHICK: I tried not to.

GARY: Eh?

CHICK: Know what I mean.

GARY: *(To MEREDITH.)* Are you Mo, then?

MEREDITH: Mo? No. I'm not Mo, love. I am Carabosse.

CHICK: And Meredith Ingram as well.

KATE: *(Waking.)* What is it? What's happening?

GARY: Christ knows. Here. *(GARY hands KATE some coffee.)* You were sleeping.

KATE: Not really. Can you... *(Get rid of CHICK and his mental pal)*?

GARY: *(To CHICK.)* Aye. Listen mate. Could you eh...I really appreciate you being here and everything.

MEREDITH: It's lucky we *are* here.

CHICK: Naw. Nothing.

GARY: When's your...eh...when are you heading back to London?

CHICK: Know what I mean. I dunno. Like, em... tomorrow. But I can stay. It's cool. No one gives a fuck. Sorry. I just want to help out. Anything I can do to be of use. I spoke to the doctor.

KATE: Tell me you didn't.

CHICK: Well. Nothing was resolved.

GARY: Listen. Em...any chance you could do me a wee favour?

MEREDITH: Yeah. He's going to do you one incredible big favour, love.

CHICK: Naw.

GARY: What?

CHICK: Nothing. I dunno, man. I'm like, know what I mean.

MEREDITH: It will be heroic. A lifesaver. Happy ever after, apotheosis, curtain. Wow.

KATE: *(A warning.)* Gary.

GARY: Yeah, I'm… *(Plucking something from the top of his head.)* … Okay. Look could you find Jackson for me? He hasn't answered my texts, no one's seen him. Could you make sure he's okay and ask him to drop in? I think Audrey would really appreciate him being here.

CHICK: *(Looks to AUDREY.)* Aye. Aye no worries. Aye. Jackson. Get him. Aye. Aye, aye. Know what I mean. That's no problem whatsoever.

MEREDITH: But, first of all… *(She puckers her lips and points to AUDREY.)*.

CHICK: Naw.

KATE: *(To no one in particular.)* Know how earlier on I was going on about the last thing I said to her before she left the house? Remember my big dramatic EastEnders speech? Turns out it was rubbish. I've just remembered that I said something else. After that. On Facebook. I wrote a comment. Told her to stop moaning. Nice, eh?

GARY: That doesn't count. Just remember your last words.

KATE: Last words?

GARY: Come on. You know what I mean.

KATE: Why don't you "just remember"? Can you just remember what she was wearing when she got in the car? Can you just remember her birthday? Can you just remember her middle name? What colour of eyes does she have? What scares her more than anything else in the world?

MEREDITH: *(To KATE.)* Why did you tell her to stop moaning?

GARY: Who are you? Chick…fuck sake.

KATE: *(To GARY.)* Please stop swearing in here! It shouldn't be like that. *(To MEREDITH, but for herself.)* It was a joke we had about my friends on Facebook. Audrey always said my pals just seem to use it to moan about how tired they were or how they hate their job or how they were looking forward to getting drunk or how their kids were driving them crazy. She said reading my Facebook was like getting ten daily haiku suicide notes. So, I was taking the mickey that's all. She was saying she felt a bit down and I took the mickey.

GARY: She would've laughed Kate, c'mon.

KATE: See, I had her young. My pals are having their children now. So they're older and they get tired. It is difficult. And they also had a life before the baby: a job, romances, ambitions, which they have to pause, or juggle or give up on completely; so a lot of them feel, I dunno… scared I suppose. But it's hard because you'd think I would be the person they would come to then, these mothers, to ask for help or advice, but I'm not. And that's not because I was young and it was a long time ago – it is that, but it's not *just* that – it's that they're all being so hippy about it all. And I was a fascist mum. In their eyes anyway. I was young and fast and I knew what I wanted. I set rules and I could tough it out. Now they're all, "oh children in Chad sleep on their mother's face until they're twelve". And…I just want to say to them…but what are the grown-ups in Chad like? Paragons of excellence? Are they the ultimate grown-ups? They'd better be. Because you're not raising a child, you're raising a grown-up. All your decisions are about trying to shape a grown-up who is kind and clever and whose company

you love. All the other stuff is just…justification.
Because they might think they're being cool
and hippy and 1960s but they're a decade out.
They're more like the housewives of the 50s
than the 60s. They're becoming the type of
women their mothers rebelled against. And it
doesn't matter how many cakes they bake or
outfits they knit. They can sacrifice their entire
existence to their childcare theories but they'll
never be as close to their kids as I am to Audrey.
As grown-ups. Never. It's a pretty safe bet their
daughters will be disgusted with their choices. But
they'll get the chance to find out… and I won't.

(A big silence. Then…)

MEREDITH: *(About CHICK.)* This guy is going to save your
daughter's life.

FIVE: THE LILAC FAIRY

Can this be right?

Chick is in a graveyard with Mo.
This is London in the middle of the day.
They're drinking.
Swaying on their feet.

They are not close.

MO: So what would happen then?

CHICK: Just…I dunno. Normal stuff.

MO: Where would we stay?

CHICK: Maybe, like…a hotel.

MO: I've stayed in hotels before.

CHICK:	I think it's in a hotel. We could stay in the hotel it's in. Just like, hingme. Go up the stairs at the end. I could say, "naw, Mo had to go up early. She was a bit tired. I'd better go up. Check on her." And all that. Know what I mean.
MO:	*(After a bit of thinking time.)* No.
CHICK:	How no?
MO:	I dunno.
CHICK:	I just think, like…if you were away from here it might be…
MO:	What?
CHICK:	There's a ceilidh as well.
MO:	I don't know nothing about all that.
CHICK:	No. I know. But. It's not a, know what I mean, there's no church. It's on a beach or something.
MO:	I've been to beaches.
CHICK:	But…but we could be all dressed up. And we could walk with all the others. We could hold the glass of champagne they give us and not even drink it. Just hold it. There's bound to be a big fire. We could totally sit there and look at it. And kinda like hingme…kinda…You just have to listen. Just stand there listening and you get a feeling. I dunno. It's a comfort hing int it?
MO:	How far is Scotland?
CHICK:	It's…I dunno.
MO:	It's like really, really far.
CHICK:	It's not. It's…it's one long day away, that's all.

MO: What if someone's camera got nicked?

CHICK: It'll no get nicked. I'll keep an eye on it.

MO: Not my camera! Some other cunt! I don't have a fucking camera!

CHICK: I dunno then.

MO: They'll come to me. They'll point the finger. What will you do then? What if they want to go through my bag? What will you do?

CHICK: Well...how...don't...try not to steal any cameras.

MO: I haven't fucking touched their fucking cameras! You're fucking as bad as them!

(Big silence.)

MO: How could we even afford it?

CHICK: I can get the money.

MO: How?

CHICK: My mum has, like, money put aside. If I'm going up to see Gary and Jackson for a reunion or that, she lets me have some of it. See for a wedding... we'll have all we want.

MO: Is she rich then?

CHICK: Aye. My dad is, but he's ill.

MO: What's up with him?

CHICK: *(Shrugs.)* Loads of stuff. Blood mostly. He's been ill since my eleventh birthday. You can't move him and if he speaks it's like that... *(He does a hoarse whisper.)*

MO: Ha ha ha !!! Is it?

CHICK: He had potential. That's the tragedy. He would've changed the way things are. People say that all the time. You're not even really allowed in there. I go in sometimes. There's a place you can stand and he doesn't know you're there. In the corner. You can just stand and watch him. But he's gonna die. Any day now. I'll probably get some of the money when he dies. Set myself up. I dunno. Maybe.

MO: Who says there's going to be a fire you can sit at?

CHICK: I can get you a dress too. And a shawl. Beautiful wool. And if you want to walk back to the hotel, along the shore, you can look back over your shoulder and I'll be by the fire, waving. And I can blow you a kiss. Like this. *(He blows a big, exaggerated kiss…)* And you'll know that I'm always there. And that we're connected.

MO: It don't even matter if it's raining does it?

CHICK: Naw. Sometimes, on a beach, it's even better when it's raining.

MO: It would still be alright.

CHICK: I know! That's what I'm fucking hingme. Know what I mean.

MO: If you've got all this money we should bring Edward and Sammy F with us in all.

(Beat.)

CHICK: Naw. Nah. No way. That's…no it.

MO: It would be a laugh innit. All of us on the bus. Down the beach. That's a giggle that.

CHICK: No! And we're going on a train not on a bus! We'll be drinking wine from plastic cups on a

train, reading magazines, looking at the towns
and mountains. Me and you. No...fucking...
Edward or Sammy F. No.

MO: I'm not going then. Fuck that shit.

CHICK: Oh come on tae...

MO: What? Why would I want to go and stand on a
fucking beach in fucking Scotland with people
who...why they even getting married on a
beach? It's not normal. When is it?

CHICK: A month or something. Time to get it all...know
what I mean. All I've got to do is ask them if it's
okay. But it will be. They're my best friends.

(A big silence.)

MO: Were you there when I got glassed?

CHICK: Aye.

MO: All that stuff he was saying about my baby. That
ain't true.

Who's that shouting in the distance?

It's Meredith.

She's bringing drinks from the bar.

*They're in that hell-hole boozer across from the hospital.
Chick is sitting a table in the corner.*

MEREDITH: *(As she sits, to some unseen arsehole at the bar.)* Oh
that's very original I must say! You're quite the
wit! And if we did, do you know what would
happen? You would be unable to perform.
When it comes to the crunch you will be sitting
on the edge of my bed, flaccid and weeping I

can practically guarantee it. So let's spare each
other the pain and end this before it even begins.
Yeah, cheers. *(For CHICK.)* Prick. I normally
would as well, but I feel we're on the trail of our
fate here, and time is an issue. *(She drinks quickly,
joylessly.)* Right love, it's very straightforward. We
have to treat the current situation as if it were
the story of Sleeping Beauty. That's our way out.

CHICK: *(A little harried.)* Know what I mean. Right, just
neck this and go. Right? Find Jackson. That's the
most important thing sure it is?

MEREDITH: No. We need to get the roles straight first. Okay,
we know Princess Aurora, that's carved in stone.
We also know who the King and Queen are -
Mr and Mrs in there – true fact. And of course,
we know the dreaded Carabosse... *(She strikes a
pose.)* The question is...are you the Handsome
Prince "Desire", or are you not?

CHICK: I am. *(He's finished his drink.)* Shit. Drank that too
fast. One more as a sharpener, okay, then we
go. *(Getting up and going to the bar.)* No hanging
about. This is important.

MEREDITH: *(Continuing.)* I think it's pronounced "Deseree"
but that doesn't sound like a Prince to me. It
sounds like a wee girl on the X Factor who
wouldn't make it to Boot Camp. God there's the
fairies too! I can't remember their names. They
each do a party piece and it takes for bloody
ever. They give the baby Princess attributes like
Grace and Wit and Music and Dance and Beauty
and...I dunno...an Xbox and...Thanks, love...

*Chick is back from the bar with a collection of drinks
– shorts and wine.
He has a system for drinking under the clock
A system Meredith seems familiar with.*

Chick drinks.

And Chick knows.
It's poison now.
Tonight it's just poison, man.
He's been told a million times.
He was told in that hospital back in London.
And he believed it.
But now he can feel it.

Sometimes it's a sharp, cutting pain...
Echoes of the toothache-gone-wrong that got this whole fucking thing started
Climbing up through his jaw, electrically.
Seeping its toxin between his skull and his brain, all yellow and burning acid.
Then there's the flickering shutdown of function: sight, limbs, thought
Off/On. Right/Wrong.
He's rolling on a harbour wave of nausea.
Sometimes there's blood in his mouth.

It's worse now than it's ever been.
Getting worse with every sip.

But Chick drinks.

MEREDITH: *(Finishing her first drink.)* Oh fudge, the Lilac Fairy! She's a big part too. She's the one who arrives late so she hasn't had time to give her present. Of course she can't cancel out my curse (I wanted the baby to die) but she can temper it.

CHICK: How...em...how come you want the baby to die?

MEREDITH: Because I wasn't invited to the Christening!

CHICK: I didn't get invited to Gary and Kate's wedding.
            In the end. *(He knows this isn't true…)* Kate didn't
            want me to ruin it.

(Beat.)

MEREDITH: Really? So…now…wait a minute then. Who does
            that make you now? Me? Are you Carabosse?

CHICK: No. I'm the fucking…hingme…Handsome
            Prince. Know what I mean.

MEREDITH: Well, maybe not, love. Could you be The Lilac
            Fairy I'm wondering?

CHICK: No.

MEREDITH: A latecomer? A dizzy head? Someone with the
            power to change the curse from death to one
            hundred years of sleep? It has to be considered a
            possibility.

CHICK: Naw. I don't want to be The Lilac Fairy. I'm
            the Handsome Prince so I am. That's…that's
            happening.

MEREDITH: Well. We'll come back to it. And there's all this
            other stuff too…A castle covered in thorns, and
            a spinning wheel, a poisoned needle…

CHICK: *(Singing under his breath.)* "I've seen the needle
            and the damage done…" 72. Harvest.

MEREDITH: It all ends in a great big nutjob wedding. It's
            like flipping *Shrek* at the end…Puss In Boots,
            Little Red Riding Hood… it's ultra-confusing
            and not very good. The Disney version stands
            head and shoulders above anything the Latvian
            Choreographer Sim Bree has conjured up. He
            claims his finale is the "ultimate apotheosis".
            That's when everything comes together,
            everyone gets what they want and the central

character is raised to god-like status. Christ, the Latvian Choreographer Sim Bree doesn't half drag out his apotheosis. I wonder if I killed the bugger? No. I think I would feel different. Right! If we do this…follow our fate…we get our apotheosis. *(A glass.)* What is this?

CHICK: Port.

MEREDITH: And that one?

CHICK: Gin and water. It only works if you do it after the port though.

MEREDITH: *(Drawing CHICK a look.)* Tell me of this Jackson?

CHICK: He's my best friend. Like Gary. The two together. Know what I mean. I love them. You're not allowed not to love them.

MEREDITH: Is he Lilac Fairy material do you think?

CHICK: Aye. He's big. Like, muscles. Sport and stuff. Cool as…shit man…and clever. He's got ideas. Know what I mean. Boof. He owns a hingme. One of they places.

MEREDITH: What? A bar?

CHICK: No, for kids. Babies and toddlers and that? Everything's soft and slidey.

MEREDITH: A soft-play area?

CHICK: Aye. It's called Castleland. All done up with like, dragons and cannons and…shit man…he's the handsome prince sure he is?

MEREDITH: Yup. Nae luck Lilac. *(She downs a drink and something catches her eye which makes her freeze.)* God.

CHICK: What?

MEREDITH: Look.

Look.

Mr Ingram sits in the opposite corner.
He has an untouched gin and tonic on the table.
He's terrified of this place.

Meredith gets up and goes to his table.
Chick moves his drinks and coat over to Mr Ingram's table too.
It's all very awkward for him.
What's the social procedure here?

MEREDITH: *(To Mr Ingram.)* You don't even like pubs.

For just a second Mr Ingram thinks he must be seeing things.
But he lives in the real world.
If you can see it, it's there. That's all.
So he gathers himself quickly back together.

MR INGRAM: Why are you dressed like that?

MEREDITH: If you don't know by now, I'm not going to tell
you. Is the Latvian Choreographer Sim Bree
dead or alive do you know?

MR INGRAM: Your latest victim.

MEREDITH: Jesus Christ. *(To Chick.)* Sorry about this.
My brother is scoring points. The Latvian
Choreographer Sim Bree is my *only* victim.

MR INGRAM: No. No he's not.

Now he sees Chick.
Recognises him.

MR INGRAM: Oh yes. Of course. Yes. You two together. I see
the angle. *(To Chick, really looking now…)* You're a
very sick man of course.

CHICK: Awright. You okay for a drink?

MR INGRAM: *(To MEREDITH, about CHICK.)* This guy needs to get back to the hospital. You should never've dragged him away.

MEREDITH: He's not a patient, he's a visitor. What are you doing in here? How's Sim Bree? Dead? No. Is he?

CHICK: We're just going, know what I mean. The clock is ticking an that. One more and we're shooting off. Sure we are? Quick one.

MR INGRAM: *(Looking closely at CHICK.)* You have, what, poisoning, or…?

CHICK: Ach naw. Toothache, so it is. Know what I mean. Infected and… but fine now. Cool. In a way. So it is.

MR INGRAM: Okay. Dangerous game though. When the system is ridden there's a very real chance of developing…

CHICK: *(Standing. Harder…)* You wanting a drink or not?

MR INGRAM: Oh, I think everyone seems to have had quite enough to drink. Especially you. *(Without any real concern.)* Do you have a rash? Have you checked? How's your vision?

CHICK: Nothing. Quick one?

MR INGRAM: Keep going with that stuff and you're done for matey. And that's no exaggeration. But you know all that I dare say. The wrong drink, the wrong drug and… *(Sighing, standing, reluctantly taking Chick's arm.)* Come on. I'll find someone who can…

CHICK: *(Pulling free.)* No! No. We've a task. Tonight. Heroes an that. No one saves me tonight – I save them! *(To MEREDITH, desperately.)* Right? Sure I do?

MEREDITH: *(To MR INGRAM.)* Is Sim Bree dead or alive? You have to tell me!

MR INGRAM: You know fine well he's bloody alive! The only time you've ever listened to me was the night I went through the dosages and their effects. You know exactly what you're doing. *(Beat. Change.)* I've spoken to Hannah. You can't come home. We don't want you in the house any longer.

(Beat.)

MEREDITH: *(A little shaken.)* Oh well. Is that true?

MR INGRAM: Yes.

MEREDITH: And Hannah said that did she?

MR INGRAM: Yes. She can't take it anymore. Neither can I. As of tonight you are to go…somewhere else.

MEREDITH: What about…?

MR INGRAM: In a few minutes, when I have somehow summoned the strength – or perhaps I mean weakness – I shall walk back across the road into my place of work and begin the process of cleaning up your mess. It will be an action, or a series of actions which will compromise everything, of course. A life's work on the line. Again.

MEREDITH: *(For CHICK.)* We're very close. We share an almost supernatural bond.

MR INGRAM: No, Meredith, we don't. We share a father and that is all.

MEREDITH: Well. Is this not the worst thing you've ever heard?

Meredith seems very shaky, upset
Barely holding it together.
Mr Ingram is trembling too.

Everyone in this place is on the edge of something.

MR INGRAM: *(After a pause.)* I think it's important you realise that...I know what's going on. The game has always been that I am in the dark. But of course I know fine well what we've been doing. The medication I've been getting for you...that particular mixture, that particular dosage... You collect it...but you don't take it - obviously! I mean look! Instead, you stockpile them in a bag made of beads. Hundreds of little blue capsules. I know all of that. You're preparing an overdose.

MEREDITH: Nobody can say for sure what's going to...

MR INGRAM: *(Over the top of her.)* But do you understand what I'm saying here? I want you to *realise* what is happening between you and I – brother and sister. And I want you to be bloody horrified. Because *I* am! To be clear then: even though I know what you plan to do with these little blue capsules...I *still* supply them. Think about what that *means.* Knowing that little Tara will be... at the very least...damaged... I still give you... ammunition. Christ, just *think* about that! That's real horror! *(Beat. Change.)* Or not. Maybe not. Maybe I'm...reeling a little tonight...because... of course...OF COURSE...you have now entrapped some other poor soul into our disaster and maybe I'm ruined because of it. I should've seen that coming. Maybe I did.

CHICK: Me?

MR INGRAM: No. The...the chap...the...Simb, the guy over there, unconscious, drugged. I'll know his bloody name soon enough. He and I will be entwined for years to come. Maybe forever, I dunno. *(Chick.)* But she'll drown you in her sludge too. If she hasn't already. So... *(He hunts in his pockets and produces a small paper bag. He pushes it towards Meredith.)* I was going to do this later, but... There you go. One last delivery. There's enough in there. Just em...just remember that... just remember... *(He sits back down, puts his head in his hands and starts to cry.)*

Meredith and Chick watch him cry as if they are behind glass.
It's weird.

MEREDITH: *(Taking the bag from the table and talking to Mr Ingram, kindly...)* I always thought you would be the one who, one golden day, would whisper the secret of everything in my ear and set me on the right track. Once and for all. Free and clear. I can see now that that expectation was... unfair. How could you live up to it? How could anyone? Ach well. It's not your fault wee Jamie. You did your best.

SIX: THE AGE I AM NOW

This is wild!
Colour and racket and can this be right?

Castleland soft play area in full flight is like a beehive on fire.

Jackson, Gary and Chick are behind the front desk.
Gary is enjoying watching Jackson at work – stressed, pissed off, weak for a change.
It makes him laugh.

It looks like Gary and Chick have just dropped in for a visit, they've got their coats on.

Chick produces a half-bottle of vodka and offers it to Gary, for their coffee. Gary looks worried and shakes his head – no thanks.

Chick is embarrassed.
He puts the bottle back in his pocket without taking any.

JACKSON: *(On the tannoy, raging.)* If the boy in the Paw Patrol top goes up that chute the wrong way again I will scorch the earth from under him! Shock and awe don't come close buddy. Do not climb the wrong way up the chute! Hey! I'm talking to you ya little...I see you! I can see you doing that. Where's your adult? Where is your adult? *(To the others.)* Outlaws. We listened to grownups right? If we got checked or chased we shat ourselves, sure we did? These kids are little lawyers, no offence. They know full bloody well I can't do a damn thing to them. The parents are untouchable too. One woman punched a two year old girl right there. Right in front of me. She called her over, said "where the fuck's your other shoe" and whack. A closed fisted batter to the cheek. I screamed. The wee girl didn't flinch. Chilling, man. I can't tell if these kids are going to grow into a cold new breed, or if they'll be a flashback to something we thought we'd left far behind.

GARY: Did you report her? The mum.

JACKSON: Nah.

GARY: Should've. It's a crime. You could be liable.

JACKSON: Yeah but...see these folk...they actually *want* to be challenged. It gives them a chance to scream and shout and be in a soap opera for a minute or two. Then they tweet about it later…boast about it. Meanwhile all my other customers will've buggered off and where am I then?

GARY: You need to man up.

JACKSON: What like you? *(Shooting back to the tannoy.)* The balls stay in the ball pool! Anyone throwing the balls into the café will be…

GARY: Sacrificed to the Gods of old!

JACKSON: *(Shaking his head and turning back to GARY.)* There was a dirty protest in the bogs last week. Tell you that? Some little swine had smeared the word "Relax" on the wall. In shit. Manning Up doesn't solve that particular problem.

GARY: I put on a voice. Just so they know I'm in charge. "A court will constantly return to the past to attribute guilt and distribute punishment, but not me. A mediator looks only to the future. The key then…is desire". They love that bit. Everybody wants to have a chance to actually act on desire for a change.

JACKSON: Shit. There's a wee girl got into the rope zone. It says in letters this high, you have to be 3 or above. But they just shove them in and get the phones out, blind. She won't be able to get out. Chick, man, do me a favour will you? Gonna climb in there and get her out, I have to stay at the desk. *(Nothing.)* C'mon man.

CHICK: Me?

JACKSON: Please, mate. Come on. Just fly up those blocks, into the flume, through the tumblers, climb up the chute the wrong way and once you're over the rope bridge just grab her and wheech down the slide into the ball pool. Set her loose in the café, she'll track her own scent from there.

This is terrifying for Chick.
But his hand is forced.
He remembers, just in time, that he has a bottle of vodka in his pocket.
He sets it down on the desk and disappears into the soft play.
We're reminded of a fairy tale...
A child enters an enchanted forest
Alone...

GARY: Did you get that YouTube thing I sent you?

JACKSON: *(As he stashes the vodka out of sight.)* Aye, don't send me anymore of that stuff. I'm done with it.

GARY: What? Why?

JACKSON: Ach. Look. All this...*Star Wars* Lego figures acting out whatever it is, George Lucas does blah blah blah...I'm just...I'm not into it.

GARY: You're not into *Star Wars*? That's new.

JACKSON: Yeah, well, I'm breaking a taboo. The one thing a man of our generation is not allowed to say... in fact I can't even remember the last time I heard the phrase uttered...is "I've grown out of it". I *did* like *Star Wars*. But I've grown out of it. I did like Superheroes. But I'm forty. I'd like to go to the cinema and see just one film that's for the Me I am now, rather than the Me I was then. You read the reviews...5 stars for *The Avengers: Embolism,* or whatever the hell it's called. Honestly? That's our culture is it? As St Paul said "When I became a man I put away childish things."

GARY: Paul Weller said that?

JACKSON: Ha ha. Previous generations of men gave up on their childhood you know. They became men. That's why we're the way we are – dragging our comfort blanket everywhere we go. Trainers and computer games and voting for dictators to take care of us because we're all too…See when my dad was the age I am now…

GARY: Alright! Alright! Jesus Christ. Do I have to write the word "relax" in shit again? Okay here's a deal, then. I won't forward on Star Wars based You Tube clips if you promise not to send me any more Amnesty petitions about torture in… wherever it is this week. They make me feel guilty. Guiltier.

JACKSON: Do they? That's weird. Forwarding them on to you makes me feel *less* guilty.

Chick is above them.
They can't see him.
He's struggling a bit, but well within earshot.

JACKSON: *(Beat. Change.)* Vodka at ten in the morning?

GARY: He's doing his best.

JACKSON: I thought he said he was off it since his dad died?

GARY: Naw, it was since the wedding. Feel a bit shit about that still. I apologised but he was rubbered, so I dunno if it took. He went *back* on it when his old man died. Do you think he's still ill or whatever it was?

JACKSON: Don't think so.

GARY: He doesnae look well though does he? Keeps wincing. Coughing. And his skin is all…what

was it anyway? A toothache? How can it be a
toothache?

JACKSON: *(Shrugs. What else is new.)* You cannae get any
sense out him.

GARY: He'll never change.

JACKSON: I know. Quite nice though, eh? The world is
transforming but Chick will always be Chick.

GARY: Remember when we came back from Inter-
Railing and said we'd get him in Euston Station
but we'd got the date wrong. Lo and behold
though, we turn up...three days late...and there
he is!

JACKSON: *(Laughs.)* Aye.

GARY: I thought it was magic! Took me ages to work it
out. He'd just waited! He waited in a station for
three days. Three days!

JACKSON: Do you ever wonder how long he would've
stayed there?

GARY: One hundred years.

JACKSON: Aye. What did you say to him about the
wedding in the end?

GARY: I told him the truth. Kind of. Couldnae have
this, bloody junkie, whatever she is, Mo,
crashing in. I mean what would've happened?
We've never even met her.

JACKSON: If she was real.

GARY: I know. He was going to be on the same table as
my boss, I just...couldnae have it. I put my foot
down. Blamed it all on Kate though. Said it was
her idea. I...I...nah. Couldn't have it.

(Beat.)

JACKSON: Tell Audrey she can start this Saturday if she wants.

GARY: Yeah?

JACKSON: Of course. We're totally shorthanded. But warn her that terrible stuff comes fleeing out of these wee bastards at both ends, so wear something she doesn't mind torching at the end of the day.

CHICK: Hey.

They see Chick above them.

CHICK: Hingme. I don't mind working here. I can work here. If you want I mean. Know what I mean. I can work here and get a place. Move up. Help out. Work here. Get a job here. In here. Know what I mean.

Lights off.
Sound off.

Chick is alone in Castleland in the middle of the night.

Can this be right?

How did he get in here?
Panic!
He tries to move but he's tangled.
He has to drag himself to freedom.
How does he get out of here?
Fuck.

A torch sweeps the place.
Chick's instinct is to dodge it.
But it finds him in the end.

70

It's Jackson.

JACKSON: Chick? Is that you, Brother?

CHICK: *(Calmly, clearly.)* Awright? Jackson. It's me Chick. Sorry man. The door was open. We're looking for you Brother, know what I mean.

JACKSON: Right, right…calm down. And try using English. Might help.

CHICK: Eh?

JACKSON: Fuck sake. How do you get yourself…? You'd better not be sick in there, man, I swear to God.

MEREDITH: *(From the darkness.)* He's saying that we're here to take you to the hospital.

Jackson's torch finds Meredith lying sprawled on some soft apparatus.
He jumps when he gets a load of her get up.
She clutches that paper bag from earlier. The one with the pills inside.

MEREDITH: Yo. S'up?

JACKSON: What the hell are you meant to be?

MEREDITH: Carabosse the Pitiless. I've had a relatively distressing evening when all is said and done, so I'm lying here rebooting. If you must know, my brother admitted that he wants me dead and upset himself. It's made me feel very tired. It's nice lying here.

JACKSON: Sorry… who are you?

CHICK: Mate, this is Meredith Ingram. She's my…she's helping me. Gary wants you to come back with us. Know what I mean.

JACKSON: Jesus Christ. *(To Meredith.)* How did he get in that state?

Jackson is only getting slurs and grunts from Chick.
He can't hear what Chick can hear.

MEREDITH: It's quite straightforward, love. He had a few drinks and obviously the alcohol has reacted with whatever was already in his system and he's currently tipsy.

JACKSON: Tipsy? He can't speak. He can't stand up. Shit. His eyes are rolling back into his head! His skin looks all...

CHICK: I can speak. Jackson. Listen to me! I can speak. This is me speaking. How come you cannae hear me, man? And I can stand too, look.

Chick stands, or tries to.
He crashes to the floor and can't regain his balance – he's on the high seas.
He has to pull himself up on the netting.
He's in pain.
He's burning up.

JACKSON: Are you Mo?

MEREDITH: That's becoming a catchphrase tonight.

CHICK: That's not Mo. Her name's Meredith Ingram.

JACKSON: He says you *are* Mo.

MEREDITH: I'm not. I'm here to take you to the hospital.

(Pause.)

JACKSON: He's the one who should be going to a hospital.

MEREDITH: Your friend's daughter has been in an accident. She's in a...

JACKSON: I know, I know! Yeah. Well. I can't. I'm here.

CHICK: Gary wants you Brother. He needs you.

JACKSON: *(To MEREDITH, with an edge.)* You've made him like this. You, and people like you. He was gifted. He wrote poetry, he played the guitar, he was funny. We could talk for hours about I dunno, Jeff Buckley or love and yeah, okay, there was booze and wine and smoke in the air…but until people like you seeped in with your poison it was pure. He had a soul but you stole it. That there is a beautiful guy corrupted…

MEREDITH: Not by me.

JACKSON: By you and people like you! You seek him out! You're on him…always on him…

MEREDITH: *(Had enough.)* Ach, do you know what, go ahead and blame me for the criminal desecration of something pure, you wouldn't be the first – not even the first tonight, as it happens - but can I just point out that I don't know that guy up there from Adam. I'm on my own quest. I am trying to summon from the wreckage an apotheosis. Just once, before I die, I'd like things to come together for the good and to be raised to the level of a god. Is that too much to ask? So yeah, he's helping me, but we're strangers, okay? You, however, as I understand it, have known this man for years and years and years. Is it beyond the bounds of imagination to wonder if he may have fallen victim to *you?* A victim of your friendship? Could it be that you keep him like this…like a mascot for your youth, when there was wine and guitars and smoke and blah blah blah – like that's so special. Everyone had that, love! He's not a pet you know. He's not cartoon character that never ages!

JACKSON: I know.

MEREDITH: He's not some old CD you stick in when you're feeling nostalgic. He's not a Time Traveller. Dr Who in his phone box or whatever...

JACKSON: I know.

MEREDITH: He's a person! We are people!

JACKSON: I know!

MEREDITH: If *you* can change and grow why can't we? Why are *we* trapped in amber?

JACKSON: I...we...you don't fucking know anything about any of this! Who the fuck are you by the way? Why are you even here?

CHICK: Jackson Brother, no. Please...

MEREDITH: *(Cool.)* What you going to do, hit me? Manly. I am Meredith. I'm in the process of fighting for partial custody of my daughter whose name is Tarra. And the rest is...a fairy tale. *(To CHICK.)* Listen I think I'm changing my mind about the role allocation. I don't think this guy's Prince Desire after all. And that's not all. I'm beginning to wonder if the beauty lying deep asleep in a castle of thorns might be you, love? Maybe you're the sleeping beauty?

JACKSON: What is all this shite now?

MEREDITH: Nothing. You're needed at the hospital. That's all.

JACKSON: Aye. I know.

MEREDITH: But you're not going?

JACKSON: No.

Chick has made his way down to them.

Standing, just.
But the words he says are still lost to the others…

CHICK: Please come, Brother. You can wake her up.
            Blow her a kiss. If there's love, the kiss will…the
            thorns will part.

MEREDITH: *(To JACKSON.)* Do you even know what's
            happened?

JACKSON: *(Sitting down.)* She was here. She works here.
            She left from here in the car that was hit. There
            was…she left quite upset.

MEREDITH: I see.

JACKSON: No, you don't.

MEREDITH: Don't I? So you didn't reach out a paw?

JACKSON: No.

MEREDITH: There was youth… wiggling in front of you in all
            its glory – jeans ripped at the knee and skin and
            fluffy hair – and you didn't reach out a paw?

            Jackson moves towards her.
            Chick puts out his hand and stops him.

CHICK: Don't go any further, Brother. Please.

JACKSON: I haven't touched…anyone…in that way… in
            eight years. Eight years.

MEREDITH: A bachelor then.

JACKSON: Eight years. No women.

MEREDITH: No men.

JACKSON: Nothing.

MEREDITH: It's not admirable if that's what you think.

JACKSON: I'm not asking to be admired. I'm just telling you…in rebuttal…I don't do that. Ever. I don't *feel* like that.

MEREDITH: But there *was* an incident, right? Something between you and this girl which stops you going to the hospital and buggers with my apotheosis?

(Beat.)

JACKSON: She's just young. She doesn't understand how things work. All I did was tell her the truth.

Chick can't bear that.

When he looks up he sees Kate, deep in the soft-play.
Can this be right?

She has Audrey in her arms.
But this Audrey is only thirteen.
So this is a long time ago.
Kate carries her daughter effortlessly, the wrong way up the chute.

Audrey's bedroom is up there.

Everything is mixing together.

Kate lays her on the bed.

Kate strokes Audrey's hair.
She finds herself laughing a little bit.
God, are we at this milestone already? That was quick.
I was there myself only a moment ago.
Time travel is non-negotiable.
When she's sure that Audrey is okay, she leaves her to sleep.

Is Chick really going to do this?

Yes.

When Kate is gone, Chick goes into the soft-play.
He knows his way now…
Agile now.
He climbs the chute to get to her.

He reaches Audrey's room and carefully opens the door.
The light from the corridor wakes her up.
She's groggy…steaming, nauseous.

AUDREY: Who is it?

CHICK: It's…eh…it's Chick.

AUDREY: What do you want?

CHICK: Nothing. Kinda…know what I mean.

AUDREY: Is it your turn to shout at me now?

CHICK: No.

AUDREY: I've seen you like this so don't…don't you dare…

CHICK: Aye. Aye. I know. And I hate that.

AUDREY: If you're going to lecture me…

CHICK: Naw, look, hingme…

AUDREY: Did they send you up to talk some sense into…
            They don't even… *(Sitting up.)* She tells me
            too much. I can't shut her up. She thinks we're
            sisters! I shouldn't know about…like…what
            Gary's like in bed or whatever. It's fucking…
            gruesome. I'm thirteen! She says we're old
            enough to talk, she's like that, "talk to me, talk
            to me!" But when I go out and…it was my best
            friend's party, right, and she's had a really hard

time…her…bloody brother *died* you know and
okay…I drank some wine and stuff but…know
what I mean.

(Pause.)

CHICK: Look, I just wanted to hingme…when they were
shouting at you down there…and this isnae any
of my business, like, so don't hingme. Don't
tell them I was…Naw…it was just when you
said…did you say you were drinking Strawberry
Wine?

AUDREY: I didn't buy it! Her fucking brother died. Like,
years ago and she's not over it or anything.

CHICK: No, look, just… *(CHICK sits on the edge of bed and
ploughs on nervously.)* Don't drink Strawberry
Wine. The way it works at your age is that your
palate is set for sweetness, right…your whole
system is programmed to get a boost from sugar.
But see with booze, you've got to fight against
that. You've got to teach your system to mature.
And that's not easy, cos at first your palate's like
that, gadz man, gimmie some sugar. But sweet
booze will make you sick. Your stomach can't
process the syrup in tandem with the alcohol.
But your palate keeps telling you: yum, yum,
more please, more, more, more…So you get
sick really, really quickly. Before you're even
drunk. It's no fun. Also, weirdly, these sweet
wines and schnapps and that, they have a really
high alcohol content, which you can't handle
either at your age. So it's like learning to drive
in a Ferrari, know what I mean. Grown-ups only
have sweetness in tiny measure - one glass at a
time, maybe late at night or after a meal. All I'm
saying is…you're drinking the wrong drink.

AUDREY: So…what…should I drink?

CHICK: Lager.

AUDREY: But…

CHICK: No, look…I know girls your age don't drink
            lager, even the boys don't yet. But a normal
            one, Tennents or something, it's only four per
            cent. You can just about process that, in small
            quantities. So if there's a party…get a can. You
            won't like the taste, it's hard work just to get it
            past your palate, so you'll take tiny wee sips. But
            sooner or later you'll start to feel a little buzz.
            You'll only get through one…maybe two cans
            during a whole party. You'll fly a little, but you
            won't get sick. Just buy the two cans and stick to
            them. Then once you're used to it, when you're
            I dunno, 16 or 17, switch to wine. Real wine. It's
            classier, there's usually food about when there's
            wine and it doesnae make you as fat as lager
            will. But wine is much stronger so…But by then
            you'll be able to sense all those hidden things.
            Or whatever.

(A big pause.)

AUDREY: Oh my god. Uncle Chick. That is the best
            advice I've ever…You're the only one who
            understands! Why can't they tell me that stuff?!
            Thank you! You're the only one who's told me
            the truth. The only one.

It's possible that Chick has never been happier than at this very moment.

(Pause.)

AUDREY: Did your Dad tell you all that stuff? Is it what
            "real Dads" do? Cos I don't know about what
            real Dads do.

CHICK: Nah. Neither do I really. My old man is ill. He
            didn't get a chance to do what everyone said he

was going to do. So…it's the waste that makes people sad. Know what I mean. He told me about *his* dad though. My grandad. They lived in the middle of nowhere, right, and they were poor, like, a cottage and no…I dunno…stuff. Anyway my grandad was hard as nails. He'd rage and smash the place up. When my Dad was eighteen he fought back. Knocked him unconscious one Saturday night when Grandad went for their dog with a poker. From that day on all Grandad could talk about was getting my Dad out the house. "When's he leaving?"; " You should've left home by now" and all that. Know what I mean. Then it was time. The day came and my Dad left home. Grandad didn't even say goodbye to him, just slammed the door. Dad had to walk into the village. Get a bus to a town with a station. Then it was a train to Glasgow and then a train to London. When my Dad got to London, he was in Euston Station, shit scared, know what I mean. Looking round and round, like you do that first time. And he catches a glimpse. From the corner of his eye. It was his Dad. My grandad. He was there! Ducking behind a timetable. He must've followed Dad all the way down. Dad didn't go over, didn't speak to him. He just carried on, on the Tube, to his digs. He didn't know how long Grandad was on his tail. He didn't look back, just in case he caught his eye and broke the spell. And when he went home, back to the cottage, years later, they never mentioned it. But to get that next bus…to make the connections…Grandad would've had to have left *immediately*. He must have slammed that door, gone to window, watched his son go round the corner… and just…followed his tracks.

That was a bedtime story for Audrey.
She's asleep.

Chick should go now
But he can't...

CHICK: We all have the same name. They called
my grandad Charlie Sonata. They couldn't
pronounce his real name in the village see. Then
my dad was called Charlie too, and he inherited
the nickname. That happens in wee places. So
he was the next Charlie Sonata. I kinda wanted
folk to call me Charlie Sonata. But I was Charles
at school. Couldnae shake it. Then when you
go to Uni you've got this little opportunity to
get a new name. All these folk asking who you
are, you can say whatever the hell you want,
they don't know. So I said I was Charlie Sonata.
I dunno, but... No one ever called me that.
They all called me Chick instead. Chick wasn't
my idea. I'm Charlie Sonata. Inside anyway.
(Beat.) Sometimes I look over my shoulder.
To see if there's someone there. Know what I
mean. *(Directly to AUDREY.)* If *you* look over your
shoulder there *will* be someone there. It'll be
me.

Audrey wakes a little...she holds his hand.

AUDREY: Charlie Sonata.

She closes her eyes.
He really doesn't want to, but Chick leaves her to sleep.

SEVEN: APOTHEOSIS

The lights click on, circuit by circuit...
Revealing the stage of the Latvian choreographer Sim Bree's production of
Sleeping Beauty.

Look at this place.
Gilded and grand, ornate...imposing.

It's like a kind of heaven.

The set looks pretty traditional
Almost storybook in its flat, old-school painterly style.
The castle is centre stage, partially hidden by sliding trucks…
A forest of thorns.

Meredith comes on to the stage almost carrying Chick.
God, he looks ill now. He's been very sick. It's all down him.
Meredith has other things on her mind. She sits him on the stage.
He falls flat.
He pulls himself up to his knees.

She has a quick check in the wings to make sure they're alone
Then she moves the thorns away and disappears into the castle.
She has dropped the paper bag containing the medication in the centre of the
stage
Right next to Chick.

MEREDITH: *(Appearing from the castle.)* One of the upsides of the occasional illicit sexual interlude with the Latvian choreographer Sim Bree is that he likes to be clandestine. As such, we performed our rituals almost entirely in the middle of the night and in total blackout. The upside in question being that I have all the security codes at my fingertips. Handy for decontaminating crime scenes. The cleaners will be in soon so we should get a move on. *(She disappears again into the castle. She reappears.)* Nothing.

She starts to wipe down the castle with her costume.
She pulls off the wings and starts with them.
She pulls other parts off too as she goes.
Soon, she's more or less out of costume – just a leotard.
As that process goes on, her mind clears slightly.

MEREDITH: *(Starting agitated, but settling...)* I knew they'd be
nothing there, but best to make sure. Get rid of
the giveaways. No doubt there'll be DNA and so
on scattered asunder, but there's nothing I can
do about that. If we have learned anything from
this age it is that we can wipe away fingerprints,
but genetics are immortal.

CHICK: Jackson. Jackson! Where are you, Brother?

MEREDITH: He's not coming, love. Remember? It's just
us. We're going back to see your friends at the
hospital, don't worry. It was just when the taxi
passed the theatre, I thought, goodness, here's
my chance to double back, fix the past and
prepare for the future. *(Looking things over. Feeling
calmer now, as if coming to the surface.)* There's no
evidence of anything here. Not a trace.

CHICK: No...the thorns will part...the time will come...

MEREDITH: *(Kindly.)* I know. That's what I'm doing, love.
I'm doing that now. And I know you may
think, "now hang on a minute here, Meredith,
I thought you were planning to kill yourself?
Is that not the meaning of the pills in the bag
and the broken brother? What difference does
it make if you are accused of poisoning after
you've done yourself in?" Well. You know
what...I'm not ...100% sure it was ever really
going to happen. It was something to comfort
me, strange as that may sound. That's all. I'd
think, "well, if this Tarra thing goes wrong then
at least I have death as an option". Maybe Jamie
knows that? Do you think? Is this all a double
bluff? *(Pause. She thinks not.)* It does make a
difference. What people think of you when
you're gone. I don't know why it does, but it
does. *(Standing back to admire her work. Different
now.)* Well. Latvian choreographer Sim Bree...I

83

hardly knew thee. And, as luck would have it, you didn't know me either. If he ever comes to, he'll swear blind it was lovely Leanne who shagged him in the castle as per and poisoned his wine and there shall be no evidence to the contrary. So. I do not exist. Again. Which is fine by me. Fine.

CHICK: Where's Jackson? He has to…sure he does. We've to take him to the hingme an that. Know what I mean.

MEREDITH: *(Seeing him.)* Christ, you're not doing so well, love. You're bleeding.

> *Oh it's more than that.*
> *Chick has a spasm of white pain.*
> *Inside he's on fire.*
> *He's shaking now.*

MEREDITH: Yeah, I think the sooner we get to the hospital the better. Okay? I'll get a taxi. Just…just lie there. Don't try to move.

CHICK: The thorns will part…

MEREDITH: *(On her way off.)* Yeah. Yeah. *(She stops and turns back.)* I'm just wondering if I wasn't going a little fast tonight? That's another thing. I think, maybe I have been a tad manic? It happens. And it can be hard to spot when you're in the throes of it. Because I have to be honest…standing here, having wiped down a crime scene and seeing you bleed and…well, everything…I'm just a little confused as to how it's all…supposed to work. In the end. You know…in real life. The *Sleeping Beauty* stuff. It's not straightforward is it? I wonder if I haven't perhaps…led us both on a merry dance?

CHICK: No! It's gonna work! It will work. Everyone will
            get what they want. Fucking…Apotheosis! Know
            what I mean.

> *Chick has a blast of pain in his gut.*
> *Red this time.*
> *He writhing now.*

MEREDITH: Shit. *(As she exits, in panic.)* Taxi, taxi, taxi, taxi,
            taxi…etc.

> *Chick lies centre stage.*
> *The paper bag is beside him.*

> *And things change.*

> *It's like when it starts to snow.*
> *You can feel it coming.*
> *Then before you know it,*
> *And without being able to say exactly when it began,*
> *Snowflakes are everywhere.*

> *Well…*
> *The Fairies are everywhere.*

> *The ballerinas dance towards him exquisitely, delicately…sincerely.*
> *They have gifts for him.*
> *They hope he likes them.*
> *They hope these gifts will help him.*

> *They lay their gifts at his feet*
> *And one by one kiss him gently on the cheek.*

> *Last to arrive is Carabosse.*
> *She has a gift too.*
> *This is the gift she would have given to the Princess*

Had she been invited to the christening.

*As Carabosse approaches Chick, the other Fairies pull back.
They're scared.*

He's not.

He takes the gift, and thanks her.

Can this be right?

Is he really going to do this?

*He's not sure.
Chick counts to three before he opens the gift*

And in he goes

Into a consult room in a new hospital.

*There is no personality here.
This room belongs to whoever is in it.*

Mr Ingram is in it.

*Chick is different now.
He holds himself upright.
He's confident, articulate…awake.*

MR INGRAM: *(On the phone.)* I want you to know that I don't
recognise you. I've seen you. You stand in the
corner. You thought that if you stood in that part
of the room I couldn't see you, didn't you? But
you were wrong. I could see you. I just didn't
recognise you. I know you're my flesh and blood.
They tell me that. But I just don't see it. I've

never seen it. You're a stranger in the crowd to me.

Chick's heard those words before.
Of course he has.
His father whispered them in his ear…
Just before he died.

MR INGRAM: *(Seeing Chick.)* You can't be in here.

CHICK: Who were you speaking to? On the phone?

MR INGRAM: No, we're not doing that. Out you go.

CHICK: I wanted to ask you something Doctor? Just one, quick thing. I wonder…is there anything that you're not telling us here?

MR INGRAM: No.

CHICK: Anything at all? Because I don't know if I've made it clear just how important this is to me. It's everything. Absolutely everything. Do you understand? It's the one thing I would like to do. The only thing I've ever wanted to do.

MR INGRAM: There was nothing else. And you can't be in here.

CHICK: Yeah. She's sixteen years old though. She's looking over her shoulder, right now. And do you know who she's looking for?

MR INGRAM: I have no idea what you're talking about.

CHICK: She's looking for Charlie Sonata.

MR INGRAM: Are you a relation of eh…ah…ah…?

CHICK: I was just wondering…isn't there some kind of…? I dunno. I suppose I'm asking if there is a procedure…a transfusion. Something from me that can go to her. A lifesaver. Do you know what I mean?

MR INGRAM: No. Well. No. Not really. Well. It's…

CHICK: Doctor. Please. Tell me.

MR INGRAM: It would mean giving everything away. You understand? It would be non-negotiable.

CHICK: I know that. When I saw Audrey in that big bed…At first I thought there was like…something missing. Something important. Maybe it was there once, but it isn't there now. But actually it *was* there. Sure it was Doctor? It was me.

MR INGRAM: It has to be your choice.

CHICK: I know.

MR INGRAM: A deliberate action.

CHICK: I know. I can do it.

Dr Ingram takes the paper bag and gives it to Chick.

The Fairies return to sweep Chick back to centre stage of Sleeping Beauty.

Things have changed again. It's a little mixed up.
The soft-play has seeped into the set of the ballet.
As has Audrey's bedroom, which is now, also, her hospital room.
Gary and Kate are by her bed, holding Audrey's hand.
Jackson comes into the room. Gary is pleased to see him.
He takes a seat at the bedside.
The phone box is in the shadows. Mo is inside, waving.
Mr Ingram has returned to his seat in the corner of the pub,
where he dries his tears and takes a drink.

The thorns have taken over the world.

Chick opens the paper bag and calmly takes the medicine.
All of it.

As he does so, he nods to the Fairies
And they take back their gifts...one by one...
And sadly fly them to Audrey.
They leave them piled by her bed.
They are unseen by Jackson, Gary and Kate.

As this is going on Meredith enters. She gasps when she sees Chick.
To us he looks fine - maybe even better than he's ever looked.
He's sitting up, awake.
But what Meredith can see is someone on the very verge of death.
She sees the bag in his hand and knows exactly what he's done.
She holds his head.
When she puts her hand to his mouth it comes away covered in blood.
She's about to run off, call for help when he takes her arm.

He pulls her towards him and whispers something in her ear.

These are his last words.

They have a powerful effect on Meredith. She can just about mouth
..."Wow".
These are the words she needed to hear. She takes a deep breath.
She smiles.
Then she pulls herself together and runs off for help.

Carabosse is the last to take back her gift.
She flies to Audrey's bedside, towering over her...
With menace
She spreads her black wings wide.

But Chick isn't scared.
He knows who he is and he knows what he's doing.

Chick is the one who doesn't change.
Chick has a soul the size of a buffalo's heart.
Chick is a guard dog.
And if he has to, he can wait for a hundred years.

He blows Audrey a kiss…

And blows Carabosse away.

It's a gust that sweeps over all the characters…

The Fairies are gone
And the thorns disintegrate to nothing.

The instant they vanish we see Chick as he really is:
Sprawled horribly, propped up on the stage,
Glassy eyed, bleeding, shuddering.

We see his face. And Audrey's face.

That's all there are now…two faces.

Slowly, slowly Chick's eyes are closing.

Slowly…slowly…

And although all we can see are two faces, balanced, almost motionless…
It feels like the peak of a crescendo, held at an almost unbearable volume.
Unbearable until…

Chick's eyes close.

At that very moment Audrey's eyes shoot open!

She springs up in bed gasping for air.
The people around her explode from their seats.
It's panic, pandemonium, celebration, emergency...

Audrey is alive

But Charlie Sonata is dead.

THE END

WWW.OBERONBOOKS.COM

Follow us on www.twitter.com/@oberonbooks
& www.facebook.com/OberonBooksLondon